The Sisters by James Shirley

A COMEDIE.   As it was Acted at the private House in Black Fryers.

James Shirley was born in London in September 1596.

His education was through a collection of England's finest establishments: Merchant Taylors' School, London, St John's College, Oxford, and St Catharine's College, Cambridge, where he took his B.A. degree in approximately 1618.

He first published in 1618, a poem entitled Echo, or the Unfortunate Lovers.

As with many artists of this period full details of his life and career are not recorded. Sources say that after graduating he became "a minister of God's word in or near St Albans." A conversion to the Catholic faith enabled him to become master of St Albans School from 1623–25.

He wrote his first play, Love Tricks, or the School of Complement, which was licensed on February 10th, 1625. From the given date it would seem he wrote this whilst at St Albans but, after its production, he moved to London and to live in Gray's Inn.

For the next two decades, he would write prolifically and with great quality, across a spectrum of thirty plays; through tragedies and comedies to tragicomedies as well as several books of poetry. Unfortunately, his talents were left to wither when Parliament passed the Puritan edict in 1642, forbidding all stage plays and closing the theatres.

Most of his early plays were performed by Queen Henrietta's Men, the acting company for which Shirley was engaged as house dramatist.

Shirley's sympathies lay with the King in battles with Parliament and he received marks of special favor from the Queen.

He made a bitter attack on William Prynne, who had attacked the stage in Histriomastix, and, when in 1634 a special masque was presented at Whitehall by the gentlemen of the Inns of Court as a practical reply to Prynne, Shirley wrote the text—The Triumph of Peace.

Shirley spent the years 1636 to 1640 in Ireland, under the patronage of the Earl of Kildare. Several of his plays were produced by his friend John Ogilby in Dublin in the first ever constructed Irish theatre; The Werburgh Street Theatre. During his years in Dublin he wrote The Doubtful Heir, The Royal Master, The Constant Maid, and St. Patrick for Ireland.

In his absence from London, Queen Henrietta's Men sold off a dozen of his plays to the stationers, who naturally, enough published them. When Shirley returned to London in 1640, he finished with the Queen Henrietta's company and his final plays in London were acted by the King's Men.

On the outbreak of the English Civil War Shirley served with the Earl of Newcastle. However when the King's fortunes began to decline he returned to London. There his friend Thomas Stanley gave him help and thereafter Shirley supported himself in the main by teaching and publishing some educational works under the Commonwealth. In addition to these he published during the period of dramatic eclipse four small volumes of poems and plays, in 1646, 1653, 1655, and 1659.

It is said that he was "a drudge" for John Ogilby in his translations of Homer's Iliad and the Odyssey, and survived into the reign of Charles II, but, though some of his comedies were revived, his days as a playwright were over.

His death, at age seventy, along with that of his wife, in 1666, is described as one of fright and exposure due to the Great Fire of London which had raged through parts of London from September 2nd to the 5th.

He was buried at St Giles in the Fields, in London, on October 29th, 1666.

Index of Contents

To the Most Worthily Honoured William Paulet Esquire
DRAMATIS PERSONAE
SCENE
PROLOGUE AT THE BLACK-FRYERS
THE SISTERS
ACT I
SCENE I - A Woody Country
SCENE II - A Room in Paulina's Castle
ACT II
SCENE I - Fabio's Cottage
SCENE II - A State Room in the Castle
ACT III
SCENE I - An Apartment in the Castle
SCENE II - An Apartment in Antonio's House
ACT IV
SCENE I - A Wood Before the Banditti's Cave
SCENE II - A Room in Antonio's House
SCENE III - A Room in the Castle
SCENE IV - The Approach to the Castle
SCENE V - Before the Castle
ACT V
SCENE I - A Room in Antonio's House
SCENE II - An Outer Room in the Castle
EPILOGUE
JAMES SHIRLEY – A CONCISE BIBLIOGRAPHY

To the Most Worthily Honoured William Paulet Esquire

Sir,

Compositions of this nature, have heretofore been graced by the acceptance, and protection of the greatest Nobility (I may say Princes) but in this age, when the Scene of Drammatick Poetry is changed into a wilderness, it is hard to find a patron to a legitimate muse. Many that were wont to encourage Poems, are fall'n beneath the poverbial want of the composers, and by their ruins are only at leasure so take measure with their eye, of what they have been. Some extinguished with their fortune, have this happiness, to be out of capacity of further shipwreck, while their sad remaynes peep out of the sea, and may serve naked marks, and caution to other Navigators, Malignant stars the while! In this unequall condition of the time, give me leave to congratulate my own felicity, that hath directed this Comedy unto you, who wear your nobleness with more security, than titles, and a name that continues bright and impassible among the constellations in our Sphear of English honour. I dare not detain you, Sir, with too long a Preface; if you please to entertain these Papers, as the modest tender of my service, I shall receive it as a most kind influence upon me; and you will engage to all your commands, the humble heart of

Sir,
Your faithful Honourer,
JAMES SHIRLEY.

DRAMATIS PERSONAE
Farnese, Prince of Parma.
Contarini, a Nobleman.
Antonio, Uncle to the Sisters.
Frapolo, the chief Bandit.
Castruchio   }
Longino   }
Strozzo   }
Rangino   } Bandits
Pacheco   }
Lucio, Paulina's Steward.
Giovanni   } Servants to Paulina.
Stephanio   }
Fabio.
Piperollo, Son to Fabio,
Countrymen.
Citizens.
Petitioners.
A Scholar.

Pulcheria disguised, and under the name of Vergerio and attending on Contarini.
Paulina   } Sisters
Angellina   }
Francescina, Angellina's maid
Morulla, Wife to Fabio.
Two Gentlewomen.
Waiting-women &c

SCENE

Paulina's Castle and Antonio's House in the Duchy of Parma and the Adjacent Country.

PROLOGUE AT THE BLACK-FRYERS

Does this look like a Term? I cannot tell,
Our Poet thinks the whole Town is not well,
Has took some Physick lately, and for fear
Of catching cold dares not salute this Ayr.
But ther's another reason, I hear say
London is gone to York, 'tis a great way;
Pox o'the Proverb, and of him say I,
That look'd ore Lixcoln, cause that was, must we
Be now translated North? I could rail to
On Gammar Shiptons Ghost, but 't wo' not doe,
The Town will still be flecking, and a Play
Though ne'r so new, will starve the second day:
Upon these very hard conditions,
Our Poet will not purchase many Towns;
And if you leave us too, we cannot thrive,
I'l promise neither Play nor Poet live
Till ye come back, think what you do, you see
What audience we have, what Company
"To Shakespear comes, whose mirth did once beguile
"Dull hours, and buskind, made even sorrow smile,
"So lovely were the Wounds, that men would say
"They could endure the bleeding a whole day:
He has but few friends lately, think o' that,
Hee 'l come no more, and others have his fate.
"Fletcher the Muses darling, and choice love
"Of Phoebus, the delight of every Grove;
"Upon whose head the Laurel grew, whose wit
"Was the Times wonder, and example yet,
`Tis within memory, Trees did not throng,
As once the Story said to Orpheus song.
"Johnson, t' whose name, wise Art did bow, and Wit
"Is only justified by honouring it:
"To hear whose touch, how would the learned Quire
"With silence stoop? and when he took his Lyre,
"Apollo dropt his Lute, asham'd to see
"A Rival to the God of Harmonie.
You do forsake him too, we must deplore
This fate, fot we do know it by our door.
How must this Author fear then, with his guilt

Of weakness to thrive here, where late was spilt
The Muses own blood, if being but a few,
You not conspire, and meet more frequent too?
There are not now nine Muses, and you may
Be kind to ours, if not, he bad me say,
Though while you careless kill the rest, and laugh,
Yet he may live to write your Epitaph.

ACT I

SCENE I

A Woody Country.

Enter **FRAPOLO**, **LONGINO**, **PACHECO**, **RANGONE**, **STROZZO**, and other **BANDITI**.

LONGINO
I Like not this last Proclamation.

RANGONE
Nor I.

STROZZO
It startled me to read it.

FRAPOLO
Did you read? tis a fault Strozzo a fault!
I'l have no theef hereafter learn to read;
Threaten us with long winded Proclamations?
We are safe within our Woods, and Territories,
And are above his Edicts; Have not wee
A Common-wealth among our selves, ye Tripolites?
A Common-wealth? a Kingdom; and I am
The Prince of Qui-Vala's, your Sovereign theef,
And you are all my Subjects.

LONGINO
We are—

FRAPOLO
And is there one so base to change Complexion,
Because we are proscrib'd? I'l be no Prince.
I have a grudging on me to be honest,
And leave you to the fear of hemp, and hunger;

Have I by stratagems so oft preserv'd you,
When you were howling out your lives, and lead
Away in Dog-couples by rusty Officers?
And are you struck dead with a Paper pellet?
Your bloud turn'd Whay, because there is reward
Promis'd to bring our heads in? I renounce you—
Land Rats—

PACHECO
Most excellent Frapolo, they recant;
A little humane frailty may be pardon'd.

FRAPOLO
Shall theeves, whose predecessors have been Kings,
And conquer'd worlds, be factious, and schismaticall?
I speak not for my self, but your own sakes,
Whose Impudence, and art in valiant theft,
Hereafter, may advance you to be Princes.

LONGINO
You have confirmed us.

FRAPOLO
You were best be rogues, and one betray another,
To get the base reward; do, lose your honour,
Live branded and be pointed at i'th' street,
There goes a Rascall that betrai'd his Prince,
Or cut the throat of his Comrade, this will
Shew well i'th' Chronicles—Stand fair you varlets,
Because we cannot tell whose heart is treacherous,
I will examine all your Phisnomies,
And in whose face soever I can find
A scandalous line, or look that may beget
Suspition of a Man that wo'not die
An honourable Rebell, and defie
The Laws, I'le shoot him presently.

LONGINO
Hang Laws,
And those that make 'em, Conscience is a Varlet;
Stand fair and shew complexions.

FRAPOLO
Ye are all valiant, honest theeve landers,
And I will be your Prince agen, and dy w'ee,
As boldly, as they dare invent—

RANGONE

Hang Cowards.

FRAPOLO
I will not have you theeves among your selves.

LONGINO
How's that, and please thy Excellence, not theeves?

FRAPOLO
Not theeves one to another; but Religious—
There is a kind of a Religion
We Outlaws must observe.

STROZZO
I never knew
Religion yet, and 'twill be now unseasonable
To learn.

RANGONE
I'l be of no Religion.

FRAPOLO
Who was so bold
To say he would have no Religion?
What man is he, hopes to be drunk, to whore,
To scope the wheels, the Gallies, and the gallowes
And be of no Religion?

LONGINO
He says right.

FRAPOLO
Yee shall be of what Religion I please.

PACHECO
Tis fit we should, Frapolo is our Monarch.

FRAPOLO
And yet I must consider of some fit one
That shall become our trade
And constitutions; hum! Silence.

STROZZO
Nay, nay Prince, take time to think on't,
Ther's no hast.

FRAPOLO
I have thought,

And you shall be no Pagans, Iews, nor Christians.

LONGINO
What then?

FRAPOLO
But every man shall be of all Religions.

RANGONE
I like that well.

FRAPOLO
Why should I clog your Conscience or confine it?
Do but obey your Prince, and I pronounce
You shall live Grandees, till the State fangs catch you
And when you come unto the Wheel, or Gibbet,
Bid fico for the World, and go out Martyrs.

OMNES
A Prince, a Prince!

FRAPOLO
Provided, that no theef
Makes a Confession at his Death, or peach
His Tribe, or make a shew of penitence,
To make the Butter-women melt, and draw
Compassion from the toothless musty rabble;
This will exclude the benefit of that Canon
Declares you Martyrs for the Cause.
Scout and discover.

[A noise within.

[Exit **LONGINO**.

RANGONE
Tis a howling voice.

FRAPOLO
What Cry was that?

[Enter **LONGINO**.

LONGINO
Of one, whose pocket has given up the Ghost,
And with the fear his body should do so,
He howles O' this fashion.

[They put on Vizards.

FRAPOLO
Bring him to our presence.

[Exit **LONGINO**.

[Re-enter **LONGINO** with **PIPEROLLO** brought in.

PIPEROLLO
Gentlemen, tis very cold, I beseech you
Do not strip my Skin off, you are not sure
I shall go to a fire when I go out of
This World; and yet as I am I confesse
I shall yield very little burn'd.

LONGINO
Knock out his brains.

PACHECO
Pistoll him.

STROZZO
Cuts throat.

PIPEROLLO
Gentlemen, hear me—I am very sorry,
I had no greater sum—but if you please
To reprieve a poor wretch, I may do you service,
And if you knew my inclination,
You would not be too Cruell.

FRAPOLO
To what are you inclin'd Sirra?

PIPEROLLO
I have been commended for a Dexterity
At your fellonious trade; for Gentlemen,
I have been a Pickpocket of a child, and have
These many years been thought a pretty house-theef
Mary I have not yet breeding abroad
With such deserving men, but I shall be
Most glad to learn, and if you please t' accept
Me to your tribe, I have Intelligence
Where money lyes hid, and very few Spirits
To guard it.

FRAPOLO

Be confident, and be cover'd.

LONGINO
Let him be one of us.

FRAPOLO
Be brief, where is this treasure?

PIPEROLLO
I have an old Father, and Mother, Gentlemen,
Please you bestow a visit upon them;
They have some Goldfinches, having new sold
A piece of Land, was given 'em by the rich
Vincenzo, Father to the famous, proud
Paulina, now his heir.

LONGINO
The glorious Daughter
Of old Vincenze? she's a Semiramis.

PIPEROLLO
The very same; if you would visit her,
I am acquainted with the house.

FRAPOLO
Wee'l take a time to think on her; to th'point,
What ready money has your Father Sirra?

PIPEROLLO
Tis but two days ago since he receiv'd
Six hundred Pistolets, I can direct
To a Cedar Chest, where the fine sum lies dormant.

STROZZO
What Servants has your Father?

PIPEROLLO
Alas none, they are miserable Hinds,
And make me all the drudge, you need not fear
The Court-du-Guard; if you please let me go
An honest theeves part, and furnish me
Wish a Devills complexion, to hide my own,
I will conduct you.

FRAPOLO
A very honest fellow!

PIPEROLLO

I do not love to be ingratefull where
I'm kindly us'd, my heart is honest.

FRAPOLO
Is he thy own Father?

PIPEROLLO
My own Father and Mother Sir, the cause
Would not be so naturall else, and meritorious.

FRAPOLO
A precious rogue, fit him instantly
With a disguise, and let him have that face
The Devill wore in the last anti-masque.

PIPEROLLO
It cannot be too ugly Sir to fright 'em.

FRAPOLO
But if he fail in any Circumstance—

PIPEROLLO
'Tis not far off, I know the nearest way.

FRAPOLO
Or give the least suspition to betray you,
Be sure you cut his throat.

LONGINO
We shall.

PIPEROLLO
I thank You Sir, d'ee think I'l be a Traytor?

LONGINO
Come first along with us.

[Exeunt **PIPEROLLO** and **LONGINO**.

FRAPOLO
You heard this fellow name the proud Paulina,
Her Chests are worth the rifling.

PACHECO
The Castle is impregnable she lives in.

FRAPOLO
Was that spoke like an understanding theef,

A true Bandit? How I do blush for thee?
Was not the Orchard of Hesperides
Watcht by a fierce, and flaming Dragon, robd?
Shall wee despair to reach her golden Apples?
Wee'l make discovery of the place, and persons,
Put it to Fate, let Stars do what they please;
Mercury is a Stronger theef than Hercules.

[Exeunt.

SCENE II

A Room in Paulina's Castle.

[Enter **GIOVANNI** and **STEPHANIO**.

GIOVANNI
What a brave time have we had, since our
Old Master died?

STROZZO
Though he were a gallant man, his Daughter
Makes his Memory burn dym, and (compar'd
To her) he liv'd but like a Hermit in a Cell,
She is all Magnificent, a Berenice,
Every hair of her head worth stellifying.

GIOVANNI
But my Lady, for so we must call her,
May be of kin to Lucifer for pride;
How many brave Gentlemen hath she despis'd,
When once their blister of Love broke out,
And they made offer of Mariage?

[Enter **ANTONIO, ANGELLINA**. They pass over the stage.

STROZZO
Here is her Sister Angellina a virgin
Of another constitution, their two natures
As different are, as the two Poles, our Mistress
Cannot be so Tyrannically proud
As she is sweet, and humble.

GIOVANNI
That's the reason her Father left her only
As much as would commend her to a Nunnery.

STROZZO
Her Uncle dotes upon her.

GIOVANNI
He does love her.

STROZZO
Tis an old blunt brave fellow; but he has
Quite lost our gallant Ladies good opinion,
He is out of grace.

[Exit **ANTONIO, ANGELLINA**.

GIOVANNI
Because he would correct her insolence,
Who oblig'd by her father to the care of
Her governour, wo'not tie up his Counsell,
Which he enforces sometimes so passionately,
It is a sport to hear her contempt of his gravity.

[Enter **PAULINA, ANTONIO**.

He has met my Lady, I see a quarrell
In their looks already, let us withdraw
Behind that Lobby, we may hear, and
Laugh securely.

[Exeunt **GIOVANNI** and **STEPHANIO**.

ANTONIO
How long have you been speechless? am
Not I your Uncle? why do you look so scurvily?
I do not think you are a Princesse yet,
And therefore take the boldness to salute you,
Without the Ceremony of Petitioners
That haunt your Ladiships charity; or if
You thought me despicable, your Sister has
Deserv'd your smile.

PACHECO
It may be so—

ANTONIO
Buffoones,
That make an Idoll of you, and can pawn
Their Souls to flatter you, should be entertaind,
And Courted to your vanity. I blush for you;

Will nothing bring you into sense of Honour
Or Modesty? I ha done.

PACHECO
It will become you;
You do presume too much.

ANTONIO
Presume? why, are
Not you Paulina am not I Antonio
Your Uncle? speak.

PACHECO
I do remember Sir,
I call'd you so, while you preserv'd your wits,
And may acknowledge you again, upon
Sober Conditions, and your Senses perfect.

ANTONIO
Sober Conditions? am I Drunk, Gipsey?
What flesh is able to forbear. Dost hear?
Thou hast drunk a Devill.

PACHECO
I did not see him in my Cup.

ANTONIO
And he has sweld thee to this monstrous pride,
More than thy Sex beside; if thou goest on
At this rate, thou wilt make Lucifer an Ape,
He must be thy Disciple.

PACHECO
The Old thing raves:

ANTONIO
Thing? what thing? thank heaven thou
Art a woman; I would beat thee into a Poltise—
When didst thou say thy prayers?

PACHECO
You know I keep a Chaplain.

ANTONIO
Thy Soul wants desperate lancing;
Ther's an eternall Ulcer in thy heart,
Ten Witches cannot suck it dry, there is
A bath of Poyson in thee.

PACHECO
I shall pity him;
A Posset, and to bed with him, his head
Does want the benefit of sleep; how wild
The good man looks?

ANTONIO
Thou art—

PACHECO
The Mistress of this Castle as I take it,
Without your Legacy.

ANTONIO
I could rail upon the dead for't; dost thou not fear
Thy Fathers ghost should haunt thee?

PACHECO
I never think upon him, and it was
His providence to leave me an estate,
To keep me from those Malancholy fancies,
And I will have you my caprichious Uncle
Know, in the Circle of these my Dominions,
I will have no Competitor.

ANTONIO
Dominions?
Was ever such an insolence? are not you
Some Queen conceald?

PACHECO
I am Independent, and sole regent here.

ANTONIO
So so,
Where's your Nobility? they are to blame
Not to attend—

PACHECO
Who waits?

[Enter **GIOVANNI, STEPHANIO**.

ANTONIO
But they do want white Staves, this is
Not State enough.

PACHECO
It shall be mended, let them be remembred.

[Exeunt **GIOVANNI** and **STEPHANIO**.

ANTONIO
She's in earnest [aside]—and
If I were worthy to advise you Madam,
Your grace should be a little more reserv'd,
And entertain none that did treat of Mariage
To your private conference, untill they had
In publick receiv'd audience like Ambassadors.

PACHECO
I like the Counsell well, it shall be so,
The next that comes shall find it my good Uncle.

ANTONIO
She's incorrigible [aside].
What if you commanded those that do attend
Your person to observe you on their knees
Sometimes, they must be humble to your highness;
I can forget my gray hairs, name, and bloud,
And teach your Servants duty.

PACHECO
The example
Will edifie the houshold, and you may,
By fair degrees rise to our Princely favour.

[Enter **LUCIO**.

LUCIO
Madam, the Lord Contarini is arrived
The Castle.

[Exit **LUCIO**.

PACHECO
He comes a wooing to me, let it be
Your Office reverend Uncle to acquaint him,
Our pleasure is to give him Audience
To Morrow in full State, until when Uncle,
Make it your care, his entertainment be
Such as becomes the greatness of his blood,
And one, on whom the Prince, we know, bestows
His speciall grace.

ANTONIO
D'ee hear sweet Niece? be not you transported;
This is no dream, the man is no mock-lord.

PACHECO
I'l be a Princess here, as you directed,
If he can humble himself to Ceremony,
Promise him honourable access, and freedom,
If the Conditions please him not, he may
Return, and leave our Court.

[Exit.

ANTONIO
Is this in Nature? well I'l follow her,
And if she be not past all shame, and senses,
I will humble or confound her.

[Exit.

ACT II

SCENE I

Fabio's Cottage.

Enter **LONGINO**, **STROZZO** binding **FABIO** and **MORULLA** bound.

MORULLA
Ah sweet Gentlemen, we are very poor,
And have a great Charge.

STROZZO
We do come to ease you of your charge.

FARNESE
Pity my age.

STROZZO
You must then pity our youth.

[Enter **PIPEROLLO** visarded with three bags.

PIPEROLLO
Here, share and share like.

MORULLA
Alas we are undone.

STROZZO
What shall we do with them?

PIPEROLLO
If you have bound her hands and feet, you
May try whether she be a Witch or no, there's
A Pond in the backside, if she swim, so—
For him?

FARNESE
Have some compassion, tis our whole estate.

LONGINO
You have a Son, a pious child we hear.

STROZZO
He will not let you want.

MORULLA
Alas poor boy, he little thinks what we
With care and providence laid up for him
Should thus be lost. O pity Gentlemen.

PIPEROLLO
Boh—Lets away.

STROZZO
I begin to find a kind of a compunction,
Let us be charitable thieves for once—

LONGINO
And return half,
What say you?

PIPEROLLO
Not a gazet, y'are not such foolish thieves;
Part with present money? part with my life first.

STROZZO
Not to your Parents?

PIPEROLLO
We use them well, because we do not carry
Their Cowes away; there they have Cheese, and Butter,
Bread comes by nature, and they both can glean,

There's water in the Well too; not a penny—
If you will be so charitable, defalk
From your own shares, mine is a just thieves part;
I look for thanks, distribute your own alms;
These things must be employ'd to better uses.
Is a Father, and Mother considerable
To ready mony; oh! fie—boh!

STROZZO
Then we must over-rule you.

[Trips up his heels.

PIPEROLLO
Ah what do you mean?

STROZZO
Baul and betray your self at your own perill.
We will be bold with your theeves part—
Come neerer—Look you good Woman,

[Gives her one of the bags.

You shall not lose your thirds, say you have met
With honest theeves; this shall suffice at present,
Which we but borrow neither, that you may not
Suspect our payment, you shall have security,
This honest man bound for't, and so we leave you.

[**LONGINO** and **STROZZO** bind **PIPEROLLO** and exeunt.

FARNESE
Tis money!

MORULLA
And left one of their fellows bound.

FARNESE
Do we not dream Wife? I dare not come near Him.

MORULLA
They are gone, I'll see his complexion;
Who's this?

[Pulls off his mask.

FARNESE
Our own Son Piperollo?

PIPEROLLO

Pray Father give me your blessing, ah—
Mother do not stone me to death with that
Money bag, I am your Son.

MORULLA

My Son? I know thee not.

PIPEROLLO

A liar, you know Mother, is worse than a
Theef; do not destroy the hopes of your Family,
Alas, I was drawn in, and made a theef
In my own defence, they swore to cut my throat
Else, do you think I had so little grace—

MORULLA

Did they so? I'l try what I can do.

[She draws her knife.

PIPEROLLO

Oh my quibibles! sweet Mother, remember
You were a woman in your days, that knew
What's what, and the true difference of things.
I am a man yet, your forgivenesse may
Make me a true man. Libbing, and hanging
Are no helps to posterity, I am your own
Sweet flesh and bloud—Oh.

[They beat and kick him.

MORULLA

Kick him out of doors.

PIPEROLLO

I thank you, this Correction may do me good;
Gently, ah gently; shall I not ask you blessing,
A twelve-month hence?

BOTH

Never.

PIPEROLLO

I wo'not.
My Mother has a deadly life with her leg.

FARNESE

Boh, you tadpole.

[Exeunt **FABIO** and **MORULLA**.

PIPEROLLO
I shall do no good o'this trade.
Now to my wits, this is no world to starve in.

[Exit

A State Room in the Castle.

[Enter **LUCIO**, **GIOVANNI**, **STEPHANIO**, with white Staves.

LUCIO
This is very fine; do not these Staves become us?
But will my Lady be thus mad, and give
The Lord Contarini Audience in such State?
She takes upon her like a very Princess.

GIOVANNI
But is't not strange her Uncle should thus humor her?

STEPHANO
He gave her the first hint, which she pursues
To his vexation.

LUCIO
But will my Lord stoop to this mockery?

GIOVANNI
He is prepar'd by her Uncle; 'twil be sport,
If she but carry it with pride enough.

GIOVANNI
Let her alone.

STROZZO
And if my Lord wants confidence—

GIOVANNI
I think her impudence will make him blush,
And put him out; I have seen a Counterfeit
With such a Majesty compose himself,

He thought himself a Prince, could frown as scornfully,
And give his hand out to great Lords to kiss,
With as much grace, as all the Royall bloud
Had musterd in his veins.

LUCIO
Some Monarch
Of Innes a Court in England sure; but when
His reign expires, and Christmas in the grave
Cold as the Turkies coffind up in crust,
That walk like Ghosts, and glide to severall Tables,
When Instruments are hoarse with sitting up,
When the gay triumph ceases, and the treasure
Divided, all the Offices laid up,
And the new cloathes in Lave der, what then?

GIOVANNI
Why then the man that kist his highness hand
O'r night, may justle him for the wall next morning,
And have it too; if he come off with all
His wits the Play is paid for, and he fit
For travell.

[Enter **CONTARINI**, **ANTONIO**, **VERGERIO**; they whisper.

My Ladies Uncle, and the Lord Contarini.

VERGERIO
My Lord Contarini expects when he
May have the happiness to present his service
To your great Lady.

LUCIO
We shall Sir acquaint her.

VERGERIO
Your Office Sir?

LUCIO
Her Steward.

VERGERIO
Yours I pray?

STROZZO
Mine, Treasurer.

GIOVANNI

Mine, Controller.

VERGERIO
I kiss your hands; this may be worth my Lords
Curiosity.

ANTONIO
For the mirths sake, my Lord be pleas'd, you may
Do an act of Charity and restore her Senses;
I'll wait on you again.

[Exit.

CONTARINI
Now Vergerio?

VERGERIO
The expectation is increas'd, her Officers
Observe the State; were your affections earnest
And I my Lord your Mistresse, I should trust
Her pride.

CONTARINI
Unless she ravish me.

[Enter **ANTONIO**.

ANTONIO
She's upon entrance, her madness holds,
Your confidence may convert her, shees my Neece
And I am sorry for it.

[Flourish.

[Enter **PAULINA** attended in State, **ANGELLINA**, **LADIES**.

PAULINA
Give him accesse.

CONTARINI
What Ladies that stands on her right hand?

ANTONIO
Her younger Sister, that does vex me as much
With her humility, as the other with
Her impudence.

CONTARINI

An excellent peece, Vergerio.

VERGERIO
Which my Lord?

CONTARINI
Madam, the glory of your time and Nation,
Whose looks do shine with Majesty, and shoot
A flame t' undoe the admirer, O call in
Some beams that wait upon the thrones of light,
Or I shall fall your sacrifice, and not finish
What my great Master gave me in charge.

LUCIO
Has the Prince a mind to her himself.

STROZZO
Tis not impossible.

PAULINA
Speak on my Lord.

ANTONIO
Gipsey, she does believe the lightning of her eys
Will blast indeed, how scornfully she squinnies?

CONTARINI
I come from the great Sovereign of hearts,
Whose glorious monarchy uncircumscrib'd,
Extends to all the habitable world,
Where ever land or lover stretch'd his arm,
Whose Scepter's not like that of common Kings,
But a bright golden shaft feather'd with sighs,
And headed with a flame, which finds access,
Like subtill lightning to the most secure,
And stubborn Cell that ever yet inclos'd
A humane thought—

LUCIO
He flies high.

GIOVANNI
Tis his arrow—

PAULINA
Speak this great name.

CONTARINI

The most immortal Prince of Love—

GIOVANNI
A high and mighty Prince indeed.

LUCIO
Tis not our Prince of Parma then?

CONTARINI
Unto your beauty Madam, that makes sweet
The breath of Fame, in his name I am sent
To offer up a Servant, rich with wonder,
And humble thoughts that honour you; who can
See those perfections and not adore
The Divine Owner? Brightness that offends
The innocent eye that gazes, is in you
The cure of blindness, and the filmes that hang
Upon the humble sight, fall off and vanish,
That it may take new life and light from you.

ANTONIO
Is she not yet ridiculous to her self?

CONTARINI
I can leave Cupids Court to live with you,
And all those bowers, where an eternall spring
Makes every flower in love with it's own beauty.
The wind whose airy wings convey all sweetness
That sense can entertain, I would exchange
But to be near your breath; and think there dwels
A harmony in your voice, above the airs
Of all those charming Birds by love selected
From every wood to be his quire. I fear
I am too bold, and may be thought to wander;
If Madam you accept my amorous vows,
Which live yet in the weak expression
Of him that honours you, time will produce
A white and fortunate hour to crown our loves
With nuptiall happiness.

PAULINA
You have relation
To the Court of Parma, your name Lord
Contarini, you have no Message from you Master?

CONTARINI
Madam your fame hath fild his Court, and he
Presents by me his Princely wishes of

Your happiness, and should he see your person,
Like mine, his heart I fear would melt into
A stream of Love and Admiration.

PAULINA
Sir, we accept in good part greeting from
The Prince, but you have no commission
To treat for him; the substance of your own
Affair will ask our pause, we will take time
To answer, which till you receive, you may
Command our Court.

[Exeunt **PAULINA, SERVANTS**

[**ANGELLINA** stayes.

VERGERIO
Proud folly!

ANTONIO
Prodigious impudence!

CONTARINI
What think you Signior?

ANTONIO
I am confounded, I'll to her agen.

[Exit.

ANGELLINA
When shall I awake?
This sure is but a dream, the Gentleman
Cannot so much mistake his time and Language.

CONTARINI
I came with Curiosity to see
Her pride so talk'd of, but my heart I feel
Is taken with an object of true sweetness.
Is't not a lovely figure? say Vergerio.

VERGERIO
If but her mind answer that fair proportion,
My Lord she is worth love, but being Sister
To a woman of such pride—

CONTARINI
I prethee leave me.

VERGERIO
She is very beautiful; my Lord is taken.

[Exit.

CONTARINI
Lady, but that ther's story for your births,
I should make judgment by your modest face,
This arrogant woman could not be your Sister.

ANGELLINA
Sir, if your expectation be not answered
With her full worth, I shall beseech you name her
With less disgrace, (our blood so neer) it cannot
Be grateful to my ear, to hear her blemishes.

CONTARINI
I was prepar'd before to meet this goodness;
These words and looks become that innocent spring
From whence they flow, vertue hath such an army
About your heart, ther's nothing can approach
Ill to betray it, or proceed from you
But warranted by honour.

ANTONIO
I know not,
But sure my Lord, you talk too fine a language
For me to understand; we are far from Court,
Where though you may speak Truth, you cloath it with
Such trim and gay apparell, we that only
Know her in plainness, and simplicity,
Cannot tell how to trust our ears, or know,
When men dissemble.

CONTARINI
By your own love
To truth, you must believe me, when I say,
Although it took beginning from this visit,
I love no beauty but your self.

ANGELLINA
You said you lov'd my Sister, and exprest
Your passion in such mighty phrase and fancie
I thought your soul had made a business on't,
Pardon the weakness of my faith if I
Dare not believe this change.

CONTARINI

Your Sister, Lady,
I came to visit, not affect, I heard,
And had a purpose but to try how neer
The wonder of her pride (pardon sweet Virgin)
Came to a truth, nor did I Court her with
The language of a meaning lover; but
Prepared by your Uncle, meant to make her see
Her miserable folly; I dare not
Present such Mockeries to you; suspect not
This hasty address; by your fair self, I love you.

ANGELLINA

My Lord, If I believ'd this, reall Courtship,
I should not entertain your honour with a
A fruitless Expectation, but declare,
Besides my want of fortune, beauty, birth,
To make me worth your love, I am already
Contracted by my Father to Religion,
Whose will I cheerfully obey, and wait
When my good Uncle will dispose me to
A Nunnery.

CONTARINI

A Nunnery?

ANGELLINA

Where for
So great an honour you pretend to me
A most unworthy maid, I'l offer up
My prayers, that you may choose a heart more equall
To your own love, and greatness.

[Enter **ANTONIO, PAULINA,** and **SERVANTS.**

CONTARINI

Nay you must
Not leave me so, we are interrupted, you
May trust me fair one with a nearer Conference,

[Exeunt **CONTARINI** and **ANGELLINA.**

PAULINA

Alas poor old man.

ANTONIO

The Old man before your borrowed Ladiship
Is bold to keep his head warm, and to tell you

You are a Puppet, take that to your titles
Of honour.

PAULINA
So Sir, none restrain his insolence?

ANTONIO
I'll make him swallow down his staff of Office
That stirs. I ha'not done. Canst be so impudent
To think his Lordship does not laugh at thee?
Your eyes the thrones of light? a brace of Lanthorns,
In which two snufs of Candle close to th' socket,
Appear like fire-drakes, and will serve to light
A traveller into a Ditch. You Madam Majesty,
And the glory of a Nation?
Tho'art a disease to Honour, Modesty,
A Feaver in thy Fathers bloud, a Gangren
Upon his name, a Pox upon thee for't;
There's one disease more, yet I have not done.

PAULINA
My Charity may invite, if these fits hold,
Some close provision for you 'mong mad men;
I do command you leave my house.

ANTONIO
I wil' not,
I'll fire the house; dost hear? thou wilt burn well,
Th'ast Oil enough about thy face, and all
Thy body Pitch, very combustible.
But I'll not be damn'd for thee, now I think on't,
And since no Counsell will prevail, I'll save
My self. Before I go, give but a reason
Why thou dost slight this gallant Lord, and squint
As if he were Groom or Foot man.

PAULINA
I'll tell you,
You would have the truth.

ANTONIO
If thou canst speak any.

PAULINA
I do esteem my self
More equall for his Master.

ANTONIO

Who, the Prince?

PAULINA
No, the blind Prince of Love, you are wise Uncle,
But I am out of Poetry.

ANTONIO
I think I were best cut off thy head, and save
The Laws a labour—Ther's no talking to her.

PAULINA
I am of your mind Uncle, you may edifie
Your charge, my younger Sister, she's not proud,
Pray take her w'ee, shee'l become the Cloister;
Go, and be mortified together, take her,
I am weary of her.

ANTONIO
And I of thee;
She shall be further off too, thou'lt infect her,
Although her foolish Father, (yet he was
My Brother) I have not power to speak
Well o'th' dead, gave thee his whole Estate,
I have a fortune, dost thou hear? I have,
And to vex thee, thy Sister shall have that,
I'll see, and I can make her proud, I'll do't;
She shall have Servants, Suters, Fidlers, Flatterers,
Fine Cloathes, and all the food that can provoke
Yo glorifie her sense; I have bags to spare,
She shall not to a Nunnery to vex thee,
I say again she shall not, wee'l have humours;
The to'ther Pox upon thee, and farewell!

[Exit.

PAULINA
I fear he's mad indeed. Let me have Musick,
This talk has made me Melancholy.

[Exeunt.

ACT III

SCENE I

An Apartment in the Castle.

Enter **LUCIO**, **PIPEROLLO**.

LUCIO
For thy Mothers sake thou shalt be entertain'd.

PIPEROLLO
An under Butler would fit me rarely,
Ther's none i'th' house that shall be sooner drunk,
Nor oftner for my Ladies credit Sir.

LUCIO
Can you write?

PIPEROLLO
And read in print Sir.

LUCIO
Art thou faithfull? may a man trust thee?

PIPEROLLO
For more than I'll speak on; trusted? I was bound
For two Gentlemen lately, that could not take up
Five hundred Pistols upon other security,
My Father and Mother knows it; I shall never
Endure a thief for a thing that I know, alas
You know I am a neighbors child, my mother
Was your good Ladies nurse.

LUCIO
Do not I know thy Mother?

PIPEROLLO
Better it may be, than I know my Father.

LUCIO
Till some Office fall i'th' house, you shall serve me,
And ride with me, to receive my Ladies Rents.

[Enter **GIOVANNI**.

GIOVANNI
Mr. Steward, yonder are the rarest fellows,
In such phantasticall habits too, they call
Themselves Mathematicians.

LUCIO
What do they come for?

GIOVANNI
To offer their service to my Lady, and tell fortunes.

LUCIO
Have they no chief?

GIOVANNI
Yes a quaint philosophicall fellow, they call
Him a Caldean, a great Schollar, they do
Not come for money like your starch'd fac'd
Egyptians, but carry things for the credit of
The Mathematiques honourably; my Lady hath
Given the Caldean her Nativity, who is to consult
With the Ephemerides, and give account how
The Stars will dispose of her.

PIPEROLLO
We shall know all our fortunes then.

GIOVANNI
The worst of his train can discipher hands,
Tell foreheads.

PIPEROLLO
And Noses.

GIOVANNI
One at the first sight did but whisper to my
Ladies Gentlewoman, and she did so blush
Through her Tiffany.

PIPEROLLO
That's no great matter, I have seen one blush
Through a Plaister of Paris.

LUCIO
How's that?

PIPEROLLO
A kind of French painting Sir.

GIOVANNI
Well said Piperollo;
I have entertain'd him; but my Lady.

[Enter **PAULINA, STEPHANIO** and **GENTLEWOMAN.**

PACHECO
The Caldean
Pleases me, I long to hear my fortune,
If it be good he shall have a reward
To cherish his great Art, and worth my bounty;
What if my Stars should frown?
Didst bid 'em follow?

STEPHANIO
They are all ready Madam.

[Music within.

PIPEROLLO
Musicall knaves.

[Enter **LONGINO**, **RANCONE**, **PACHECO**, **STROZZO**, in fantastik disguises.

A Song.
Beauty and the various grace,
That adorn the sweetest faces,
Here take their glorious throne; may he
That is the God of Archerie,
Never aim one angry Dart,
But soft, and gentle as your heart,
Court it with flame, and rich perfume,
To light, and sweeten, not consume.

PAULINA
Not the Caldean come yet? my thoughts are
Inflam'd with fierce desire to know my Destiny;
You have skill Gentlemen; but I'll expect
The judgment of your Master on my Fate;
When the great man of art returns acquaint me.

[Exit **PAULINA** and **LADIES**.

STEPHANIO
Come my friends, lets lose no time; Sir.

LONGINO
I am for you to the extent of my Art Signiour.

RANGONE
If it please you, let me peruse your hand.

LUCIO
'Tis at your service.

PIPEROLLO
Please you to examine my Palm; can you
Tell me learned Sir, what is past?

PACHECO
You know that already.

PIPEROLLO
'Twill be a satisfaction to me, if you can
Make it appear, that you know something
In that point.

LONGINO
A Fracture in the Mercuriall line, and the
Mount of Saturn ill characted! you are

[**STROZZO** picks **STEPHANIO'S** pocket.

Neer a misfortune Sir.

RANGONE
Jupiters Mount is well form'd and colour'd
A Cross conspicuous, the Suns Mount well
Figur'd, and linea solis, without any intersection,

LUCIO
Your Judgement upon that Sir?

[Enter **ANTONIO**.

ANTONIO
More Anticks yet? What Nation have we here,
Fortune flingers!

STRAZZO
You shall know yours immediately.

ANTONIO
Her house is open for these Mountebanks,
Cheaters, and Tumblers, that can foist and flatter
My Lady Gugaw; Every office open,
When Poor men that have worth and want an Alms,
May perish ere they pass the Porters lodge;
What are you Sir?

STRAZZO
One of the Mathematicians noble Signior.

ANTONIO
Mathematicians? Mungrell,
How durst thou take that learned name upon thee?
You are one of those knaves that stroul the Country,
And live by picking worms out of fools fingers.

STRAZZO
And something out of your trunks, my reverend
Cato.

[Picks his pocket.

ANTONIO
How busy the raskals are, how the rogues stink?
I'll send your Regiment a Quarter-master.

[Exit.

STRAZZO
Now to my other gamester.

PACHECO
You have been—

PIPEROLLO
What Sir?

PACHECO
In your ear—a theef.

PIPEROLLO
He has a Devil; good Sir not too loud.

PACHECO
And you shall be—

PIPEROLLO
Hang'd I warrant you.

PACHECO
Let me see tother hand.

PIPEROLLO
Shall it scape with burning?

RANGONE
You shall be a Lord.

LUCIO
A Lord.

RANGONE
Hum, yes, a Lord infallibly.

PACHECO
You shall be a Knight Sir.

PIPEROLLO
Of the thieves Order, and wear my rich
Collar of hemp; is't not so?

PACHECO
An honourable Knight, upon my word.

LUCIO [To **ANTONIO**]
A Lord—Pray give your opinion.

LONGINO
Your hand—you shall be a right worshipful—

LUCIO
One of your tribe told me I should be a Lord.

STROZZO
And shall be us'd accordingly, Lords are transitory.

[**STROZZO** picks **LUCIO'S** pocket.

LONGINO
Let me see tother hand. I marry Sir, this line
Cleeres the doubt, and markes you right
Honourable, which makes up the tother half
Of your fortune Signior, these two parallell lines
From the dexter angle to be the Mount of Sol,
Has made all plain, you must be a Lord.

PIPEROLLO
He has given you a very good reason Sir,
A man can have but half his fortune in one
Hand, and two right worshipfuls makes up
One right honourable; these are rare fellowes,
I am predestinate to be a Knight,
The Stars may do their pleasure, I obey.
This should be the Caldean.

[Enter **FRAPOLO**, **CASTRUCHIO** be whispers to the rest.

FRAPOLO [aside to **LONGINO, RANGONE** and **PACHECO**]
I have narrowly observed the Castle, and
Where the treasure lies, I know my Lady
In honour will entertain us this night, and
When they are asleep wee'l take our opportunity
To rifle her Exchequer, boyes, mean time
Let me alone to humour her proud Nature;
I will so claw her ambition.

LUCIO
In the interim, I'll put a question to
His Astrology. Sir, If you please till my Lady
Return to satisfie her Seward, and oblige him
By your Art, one of your under Mathematicks
Has given me a Comfortable Destinie.

FRAPOLO
Your hand. When were you born?

LUCIO
I know not Sir.

RANCONE [whispers]
A Lord

FRAPOLO
No Matter, Venus in the Ascendent with
Sol, being Lady of your seventh; hum, hum,
With Jupiter, designes you to be a Lord.

LUCIO
They all agree; the miracle of learning!
One question more I beseeth you Sir, I
Am to ride with my Man to receive my Ladies
Rent to morrow through the Forrest—

FRAPOLO
Go to.

LUCIO
Now I desire to know, whether we shall be
Rob'd in our return or no?

FRAPOLO
What time do you think precisely to come
Back Sir, for we should know the very minute.

LUCIO
The Money is ready Sir, and we do purpose,
In your ear—

FRAPOLO
Yes, you shall be rob'd, ther's nothing in
Nature to prevent it.

PIPEROLLO
Will they kill us, and please you?

FRAPOLO
No, they shall not kill you, they shall only
Take your money, and break your pate, that
Will be all.

PIPEROLLO
Why let 'em rob us Sir, the loss of our Money
Will be an evidence of our preferment, and you
May have more assurance to be a Lord, and
I of my Knighthood—My Lady Sir.

[Enter **PAULINA**.

FRAPOLO
Madam, the Stars shine with their full beams
Upon you, Who by me their interpreter, salute
You with a glorious fortune: For Leo's Lord of your
Horoscope in the right angle of heaven, and a royall
Fixt Sar calld Regulus, or the Lions hart, culminating
With him, and a naturall reception between Mars,
And Sol Lord of the tenth, being in the first with
Mercury and Venus in the house of honour, besides
A Conjunction of Iupiter and Luna in Pisces, in
The house of Mariage, I must give Iudgment.

PACHECO
I shall beseech your cleerer language.

FRAPOLO
You shall be Married to a Prince, it is inevitable.

PACHECO
A Prince?

LUCIO
May not I come to be a Lord then?

PIPEROLLO
And I a Knight?

PACHECO
When shall I see him?

FRAPOLO
He shall within few days visit your Castle,
Drawn hither with the fame of your person,
And bravery. I need not instruct you to entertain
Him with State and Ceremony becoming his
Excellence, but if he Court you not into his arms,
I will renounce the Stars, and say there is no
Truth in Astrology.

PACHECO
How my thoughts swel already.

FRAPOLO [aside]
She has swallowe'd it.

PACHECO
Give him five hundred Pistolets.

FRAPOLO
Do not wrong so much
One that does honour you; as I bribe not
The Stars to tell me their Decrees, I dare not
For money sell their Secrets, and if any
That have relation to me presume
To take a Julio—

LONGINO
By no means Madam—

PACHECO
I like it that no Mercenary ends
Guide 'em to flatter me.

[A Drum sounds off.

LONGINO
Is not that a March?

[Exit.

PIPEROLLO

If it entrench not too far upon your art,
This Prince, Sir, has a Name.

FRAPOLO
And rules this Province,
Fernese is a Bachelour.

PACHECO
The Prince of Parma?
My blood refines in every vein already,
Dull heavy Souls that are content to drudge
In humble thoughts.

[Enter **LONGINO** and whispers to **FRAPOLO**.

LONGINO
I Fear we are betraid;
The Countries up and marching to the Castle,
We may be all surpriz'd let us to, horse—

[Exit.

PACHECO
Deny not, Sir, this night an entertainment,
Such as my Castle yields, it sha'not spread
To receive guests more welcome.

[Drum again is heard.

LUCIO
A Drum Madam.

[Exit.

RANGONE [aside to **FRAPOLO**]
Must we not stay and rob the house to night?

FRAPOLO
Madam, my art foretells I cannot be
Safe to remain here, at my return
I wo'not baulk your Castle, i'th' mean time
Cherish high thoughts, your Stars do call you Princess,
So kissing your fair hand—

PACHECO
Make me not so unhappy.

FRAPOLO

There is no dispute with Destinie,
I take my humble leave, away! to horse!

[Exeunt.

PACHECO
This more amazeth me, what danger should
Provoke this hast, if it prove their concernment,
I must believe they do converse with Fate,
And trust to them as Oracles; a Princess?
Was not my Soul Propheticall?

[Enter **LUCIO**.

LUCIO
Madam, some accident hath rais'd your tenants,
They march in fury this way, in strange postures
And Arms, as if they came to storm the Castle.

[Enter **PIPEROLLO**.

PIPEROLLO
Madam, we are all undone, the Clubs are up,
Your Tenants are turn'd Rebels, and by this time
Enter'd the Hall; and threaten to surprize
I know not whom; But the Caldean, and
His troop are vanish'd, they foresaw this tempest.

PACHECO
What should this mean?

[Enter **COUNTRYMEN**, armed.

1ˢᵗ COUNTRYMAN
I Come on you men of lusty Chine, Dear Lady
Be not affrighted, Captain of thy Guard
Am I, thy naturall Tenant, and thy Vassall;
Where be these Sunburnt Aethiopians?
I wo'not leave one Canting Rogue alive.

PAULINA
What Aethiopians, what Canting Rogues?
Do not your Clounships know me?

1ˢᵗ COUNTRYMAN
I Know our Princess?
We honour thee, and rise in thy defence;
Where be these thieves? we heard there were

A Regiment, that came to Cheat and Plunder.

PAULINA
Y'are a Knot
Of knaves and fools, and shall repent this insolence;
You that command in chief, good Captain Bumbard,
May teach your Raggamuffins face about,
Was it your stratagem to fright my guests?

1ˢᵗ COUNTRYMAN
Your Uncle told us Madam, and commanded.

PAULINA
Was it his plot? he's still my enemy.

1ˢᵗ COUNTRYMAN
Pardon us Madam,
We came simply hither to do you service;
Kneel, or we shall all be stript out of our Tenements.

[They kneel.

PAULINA
My Uncle has abus'd you,
But this submission takes our anger off,
Continue dutiful to my Commands,
And you shall be remembred; Piperollo—

[Exit.

PIPEROLLO
I know the Buttery Madam; follow me,
It is my Ladies pleasure you be drunk,
And thank her grace ye keep your Copiholds;
Dee you bring up the rear, I'l march in front.

[Exeunt.

SCENE II

An Apartment in Antonio's House.

[Enter **ANTONIO** and **CONTARINI**.

ANTONIO
Passion o' me, it is to great an honour,

Refuse a man of your high blood and name,
That Courts her honourably? I could beat her.

CONTARINI
'Tis not impossible at my return
To find a change. I must to Court agen.

[Enter **VERGERIO**.

VERGERIO
The horses my Lord are ready.

CONTARINI
Vergerio—

[They talk aside.

ANTONIO
What a Baggage 'tis, shees all for the Nunnery,
She sha'not have her will, I'll undo my self
But I'll destroy this Modesty; if I could
But make her proud there were some hope on her.

VERGERIO
My Lord you may command, but how unfit,
I am to manage this affair.

CONTARINI
Thou hast a powerful Language, it prevail'd
On me when I first saw thee, since which time
I have not deserv'd unkindly from thee, and
This trust speaks more than Common favour.

VERGERIO [Aside]
Make me his advocate to Angellina?

ANTONIO
My Lord, if you can still preserve these thoughts
Of honour to us, leave her to my Counsel.

CONTARINI
Most cheerfully, I am not desperate;
This Gentleman I'll leave to wait upon her,
Who is privy to my Counsels, and affection.

ANTONIO
Your Lordship hath found trust in him, but that
Sha'not excuse my care, to make her know

Her happiness, and the Honour of our Family,
By meeting your commands. She's here.

[Enter **ANGELLINA, FRANCESCINA. ANTONIO** engages **FRANCESCINA**, while **CONTARINI** takes **ANGELLINA** aside.

Francescina tell me, what hope of your Mistress?
How does thy Counsell work? does she pray less
Then she was wont? or listen now and then
When thou talk'st wantonly, does she smile upon't?

FRANCESCINA
Between our selves, I put her to a smiling
Blush.

ANTONIO
What said she, tell me on thy modesty,
When she found her dear delight, the legend
Of the Saints remov'd, and Ovids tales of
Jupiter put in the place?

FRANCESCINA
She said, that Jupiter
Was a most sensual Heretick, and the cestus
That Venus wore was not St. Francis girdle.

ANTONIO
How did she like the picture of Leander,
Swimming the Hellspont upon his back?
How that of Cleopatra kissing Antony?

FRANCESCINA
She Says that Queen was none of the poor Clares,
But one bread up in black Aegyptian Darkness;
All I can say, she is not desperate,
I sing no Anthems to her.

ANTONIO
What says she to her dancing Master?

FRANCESCINA
She is past her honor; that's a precious fellow,
She'll laugh to see him gamboll with his limbs,
His head flies like a Ball about the room;
You'd think he were at Tennis with it.

ANGELLINA
Though in the guilt and knowledge of my own

Defects, to answer such an honourable
Esteem of me, I dare not yet presume
To meet it; I shall want no pious thoughts
For this so great a bounty to a poor
Desertlesse Virgin.

ANTONIO
Hang your pious thoughts
And love my Lord.

CONTARINI
Not for the wealth of Parma
Should my Cause force one cloud upon her face
Or put her eys to the expence of tears,
It shall be argument for me to hope,
If she accept this youth to wait upon her,
Who may in some auspicious hour, prepare me
A gentle seat within her heart, mean time
I leave upon your Virgin lip the faith,
Of your true Servant Lady.

ANTONIO
I'll attend you
To horse my Lord.

[Exeunt **ANTONIO** and **CONTARINI**.

ANGELLINA
Poor miserable maid,
Faln now beneath the pity of thy self;
My heart, on which so late a flame of Heaven
Stream'd comfort in my holy resolutions,
Is fill'd with love, but not of Contarini,
Whose passion may deserve anothers welcome,
I prethee Francescina take thy Lute
And let me hear thy voice.

FRANCESCINA
I can sing Venus and Adonis to you.

ANGELLINA
Any thing.

FRANCESCINA
Or will you hear the pleasant Dity
How fair Calisto first became a Nunne.

ANGELLINA

I prethee do not name a Nun, the flame
That I feel here deserves no Vestall name.

FRANCESCINA
I'll do my best to fit you,
Ther's no such tool in nature as a Chambermaid
To work upon her Mistress.

[Exeunt.

ACT IV

SCENE I

A Wood Before the Banditti's Cave.

Enter **FRAPOLO, LONGINO, STROZZO, PACHECO,** with the rest.

FRAPOLO
It was a fatall business to lose such
An opportunity.

LONGINO
My Lady was wound up so rarely.

STROZZO
We were betraid for certain; 'twas high
Time to scud, and get into our Territories;
Now we are safe in our Grots, secure as
The Minotaur, and keep the clew of our
Own Labyrinths.

PACHECO
We lost a rare design, but in my opinion,
Tis better scouting here with our heads on,
Than have 'em carryed in by Clowns at the Court rate.

FRAPOLO
The ignorant Rogues would nere ha 'sold
Them to their worth.

LONGINO
And they dare as soon venter upon Hell,
As Shoot their heads into this Furnace.

FRAPOLO

But this Claridiana sha'not scape so,
I am resolv'd to visit her again, and I am
Glad I prepar'd another expectation, these
Difficulties shall make our next attempt
More glorious.

LONGINO
Those shapes will conjure up the Bores again.

STROZZO
She does expect the Caldean.

FRAPOLO
Hang the Caldean. I have a new device
Shall scoure the Castle; and make Dame
Guinever with all her pride, thank and adore
The invention.

LONGINO
How dear Frapolo? how?

[Whooping within.

FRAPOLO
Scout and discover, Strozzo.

[**STROZZO** looks out.

STROZZO
I see but two men coming down the Hill.

FRAPOLO
Cannot their worships travel with less noise?

LONGINO
They durst not be so confident without a number,
'Tis good to be secure—

[Whooping again]

—the noise approaches,
Lets to our shells.

FRAPOLO
Do you lie perdue still.

[They all retire but **PACHECO** and **PIPEROLLO**.

PACHECO
I do not like their confidence, these may be
The enemies scouts, lets non engage to soon
For fear of a reserve. The State has threatened
To send their Vermin forth.

FRAPOLO
Obscure: close, close!

[They retire.

[Enter **LUCIO** and **PIPEROLLO**.

LUCIO
What dost thou mean?
Thou hast a mind to be rob'd indeed.

PIPEROLLO
I would have art maintain'd in reputation,
You know my Lady is to be a Princels,
And you must be a Lord, and I be dubbed,
But if we be not rob'd, I know not how
To trust the Mathematicks or the Stars;
I am afraid all the Bandits are hang'd,
A thousand Pistols should not fear to travel.

LUCIO
It is not wisdom to proclaim our charge,
Though I could be content to be a Lord,
I am not over hearty, thieves are thieves,
And life is precious, prethee lets make hast.

PIPEROLLO
Illo ho ho,
Think upon your honour, are there no Gentlemen?
No wanting Gentlemen that know how to spend
A quantity of Gold?
There is no thief in Nature.

[**STROZZO** peeps out.

STROZZO
The Gentleman
Is very merry, they that mean well, and
Have their wits about 'em, do not use
To call upon our Tribe. This is a plot,
A very plot, and yet the Coast is clear.

[Coming forward.

Now I may reach their voice.

PIPEROLLO
It wo' not be, was ever men distrest so?

LUCIO
Come we are well yet Piperollo, if
The Stars Decree our robbery, it will follow.

PIPEROLLO
I pray Sir lets sit down here, as you hope to
Be a Lord, we must do our endeavour and help
The Fates. Do but hear reason Sir.

STROZZO
'Tis my proud Madams Steward, and our quondam
Fellow thief; they were told their fortunes
To be rob'd; Here had been a purchase lost
If I had not lain perdue. You shall be
Disparcht presently, never fear it.

[He Whistles.

LUCIO
What's that? I do not like that tune.

PIPEROLLO
Hum, I am not in love with that Quailpipe.
I could dwindle, but that I have a strong
Faith in the Mathematicks Theeves and be
Thy Will.

LUCIO
If they should cut our throats now—this is
Your folly; would I were off.

PIPEROLLO
Would I were a Knight in an embroidered
Dish clout. Have a good heart Sir, ther's
No more to be said in't, let the Stars take
Their course, 'tis my Ladies money—and if
We be rob'd, we are so much the neerer to preferment.

[Enter **FRAPOLO** and the rest masked and disguised.

LUCIO

Ah, sweet Gentlemen take but the Money—

PIPEROLLO
'Tis ready told; nay, nay, we are friends;
Give us but a Note under your hands for
My Ladies satisfaction, that you have received
It Gentlemen.

LUCIO
You need not trouble your selves to tell it Gentlemen,
It is all right.

LONGINO
So, so, wee'l take your words.

PIPEROLLO
I should know that vizard, the garments
That you wear too I have seen Old acquaintance?

FRAPOLO
Does he know you? cut his throat.

PIPEROLLO
No Sir, I do not know him, nor any man, nor
My self, I was not once rob'd before, neither
Did I help any man to rob my own Father and Mother;
I knew no Cedar chest I, I disclaim it, nor
Was any man that I know left bound for the
Money; ye are all honest Gentlemen,
And I congratulate our good fortune, that you
Came so luckily in the very nick, we had carried
Home the money else in good sadness—Sir,
We are made for ever—rare Mathematicians!

FRAPOLO
What's that you talk sirra of Mathematicians?

PIPEROLLO
It pleased some of the learned tribe to visit
My Lady not long since, but they are well I
Hope, they told us we should be rob'd, and
'Tis done; blessed Caldean!

FRAPOLO
What became on 'em?

PIPEROLLO
They scap'd a scouring, for my Ladies Cinicall

Uncle, in meer malice to learning, rai 'd
The Towns upon 'em, perswading the hobbinolls
They came to rob the house; but honored
Be the Stars, they brought 'em off at the
Back gate.

FRAPOLO
They seem honest fellows, let 'em live, and
Pass.

LUCIO
We humbly thank you Gentlemen, come
Piperollo.

PIPEROLLO
And yet, now I remember, there wants a
Circumstance, my pate is not broke yet,
That was a Clause, the Caldean was a little
Out.

FRAPOLO
I had forgot. [aside] will you be prating sirra?

[He breaks his head.

PIPEROLLO
Now tis done, I thank you, dear Gentlemen,
I thank you, go forth and be a Knight;
Mathematician I adore thee, it bleeds;
Where are you Sir? all is compleat, and my
Head is broke according to prophecie. Oh
Admirable Caldean!

[Exeunt **LUCIO** and **PIPEROLLO**.

LONGINO
We have not lost all my Ladies money, but
To your plot Frapolo.

FRAPOLO
This hath ripend it, and I appear a
Blazing Star already.

STROZZO
What's the mystery?

FRAPOLO
You know I am your Prince.

LONGINO
'Tis Acknowledged.

FRAPOLO
We will in State visit the proud Paulina,
I am the Prince Farness, and you
Are all my Lords and privy Counsellors
Bear up for honour of your Prince.

LONGINO
I apprehend it, 'tis a most rare design,
She will be mad to meet it.

PACHECO
Will you marry her?

FRAPOLO
I cannot tell, there may be a necessity,
But when I ha' the wench, her Plate and Jewels,
And other sums, I have cast already whither
We must transport our selves—wee'l divide all.

LONGINO
And the wench too?

FRAPOLO
No not the wench, until I cast the Concubine;
Remember who I am, the choice of flesh
Is my prerogative; no murmuring,
You shall provide our Robes.

STROZZO
Now we are rogues to purpose.

FRAPOLO
I am your Prince, and the worst thief
A States-man.

OMNES
A Prince, A Prince.

[Exeunt.

SCENE II

A Room in Antonio's House.

[Enter **ANGELLINA**, and **FRANCESCINA**.

ANGELLINA
Where is Vergerio?

FRANCESCINA
I know not Madam.

ANGELLINA
Madam? I prethee leave that folly,
I am no Lady, call me Angellina.

FRANCESCINA
I'll call you Madam, 'tis a name in fashion,
What do you want to justifie that title?
Have you not Beauty, Jewels, Gold at pleasure?
Fine Clothes, high Food, and men as motley, as
The Ambassadors to wait? does not your Uncle
Allow you all that can make up a Lady?
Pardon my boldness Madam, I beseech you.

[Enter two **GENTLEWOMEN**.

ANGELLINA
What are these?

FRANCESCINA
The Gentlewomen were commended, Madam,
Most excellent in their Art about great Ladies;
And come to tender you their humble service.

1ˢᵗ GENTLEWOMAN
Most proud if you accept our duties Madam.

FRANCESCINA
Look you, they're proud already, they have nothing
But their trade to live on; she with the face
Spotted with Ermins, hath been late in France,
And knows the mode to a Mathematicall point,
She has the theory of Song, but lost
The practick part by sitting up a nights;
She danceth still, can talk in several languages,
And has the art of every game, to instruct
A novice Lady—

ANGELLINA

To lose time.

FRANCESCINA
And what
Age, do you think the other Gentlewoman
Carries? that simpers so? the miracle
Of Painting! she presents scarce five and twenty,
But if you credit Church Records, she numbers
But five short of threescore, Medea had
No charmes like her, to preserve youth, and beauty;
She hath the art of making eyes, new hair,
And Ivory teeth, hath skill in making fruitful,
And is an excellent Midwife; she hath cur'd
A man that had no Nose, and a Court-Lady
That had no Tongue.

ANGELLINA
These are transcendent qualities;
Since tis my Uncles pleasure, they may wait,
But not to serve me.

[Knocking within.

FRANCESCINA
Who's that knocks so modestly?
'Tis not your Dancing-Master, nor the Doctor,
They have more confidence.

[Goes to the door.

'Tis the Parsons Nephew, come from the University,
Some say a pretty Scholar, and a wit;
Hath an Ambition to kiss your hand
And tender his first fruits.

ANGELLINA
What's that?

FRANCESCINA
Some Poetry.

1ˢᵗ GENTLEWOMAN
By any means Madam, you must be flatter'd,
Great Ladies cannot live els.

ANGELLINA
Let him enter.

[Enter **SCHOLAR** with a paper.

SCHOLAR
Darling of beauty, fairest Angellina,
Thus low the Muses bow, and send by me
An abstract of your self; oh make the Paper
More white by kissing your fair hand, and with
Your breath, like a soft Western gale, perfume
These lines created in your praise.

[Gives **ANGELLINA** the paper, which she reads.

ANGELLINA
What's here?—I am
A stranger to you Sir, and to your language,
These words have no relation to me;
I pity men of your high fancy, should
Dishonour their own names, by forming such
Prodigious shapes of beauty in our sex.
If I were really what you would commend,
Mankind would fly me; get a Painter Sir,
And when he has wrought a woman by your fancy,
See if you know her again; were it not fine,
If you should see your Mistress without hair?
Drest only with those glittering beams you talk of?
Two Suns instead of Eyes, and they not melt
The forhead made of Snow; no Cheeks, but two
Roses inoculated upon a Lillie?
Between, a pendent Alablaster Nose?
Her Lips cut out of Coral, and no Teeth,
But Strings of Pearl; Her Tongue a Nightingales;
Her chin a rump of Ivory, and so forth?
Would not this strange Chimera fright your self?
And yet you take the boldness to present us,
And think we must applaud, and thank you for
Our selves made Monsters by your art; no more
Of this for shame; lose not your time and honour
In this fantastick Idoll; you will say,
The world is peevish, and not kind to virtue;
Give him ten Pistolets to cure his poverty,
There are good seeds in him and they may yet
Grow with some Cherishing.

SCHOLAR
You are enough
To vindicate your Sex, I shall not blush
To write your story.

FRANCESCINA
You shall owe me Sir
An Anagram, and a Poesy too for
My next Ring.

SCHOLLAR
You shall command my faculty,
My dearest Abigall

[Exit.

FRANCESCINA
Thank you sweet Sir Roger.

[Exit.

[Enter four **CITIZENS**.

1ST CITIZEN
Is her Ladiship at leisure?

ANGELLINA
What are these?

2ND CITIZEN
We are humble suter Madam for your Favour.

ANGELLINA
Speak your request.

1ST CITIZEN
I am a Tailor Madam
That holds intelligence with forein Courts
To furnish Ladies with new Fashions,
And I have patterns of the strangest shapes
That ever Ladies long'd for.

ANGELLINA
I believe it.

2ND CITIZEN
I have the ambition to own the name
Of your Perfumer Madam.

3RD CITIZEN
'T your Jeweller;
What think you of that Carcanet sweet Madam?
The Pearls are Orient, I have a Diamond

The Sultan gave one of his Concubines,
It weighes—twenty carats, if it please you Madam,
To wear it in the Court, and I'll attend
Your Ladiship six months hence to pay me for't;
I know your Uncle Madam.

ANGELLINA
This is his plot.

FRAPOLO
By all means take it.

ANGELLINA
Excuse me; what are you? speak your desire.

4TH CITIZEN

4TH CITIZEN
I would present you Madam with a pair
Of curious Spurs.

ANGELLINA
For what use prethee?

4TH CITIZEN
For what you please, I see all men of trade
Apply themselves to gain relation to you,
And I would be your Spurrier.

ANGELLINA
Do Ladies wear Spurs my friend?

4TH CITIZEN
They may in time, who knows what may be done,
If one great Lady would begin, they ride
Like Men already; 'tis all one to me,
So I may have the Credit of your name,
And privilege to swell above my neighbors.

ANGELLINA
When I stand, Gentlemen, in need of your
Professions, I'll send for you, i'th' mean time
You shall need no Solicitour.

OMNES
Your Servants.

4TH CITIZEN
Buy a Spur.

[Exeunt **CITIZENS**.

ANGELLINA
I prethee let me not be troubled with
This kind of People Francescina; Ladies
Have a fine time, if they be all thus visited.

FRAPOLO
You are rude and fawcy fellows to intrude
So far without my Ladies licence.

ANGELLINA
What makes thee so impatient? will they not
Be gone?

FRANCESCINA
Gone? here's a new regiment is pressing forward

ANGELLINA
What are they?

FRANCESCINA
Beggers.

ANGELLINA
How?

FRANCESCINA
And tell me I abuse your Charity,
To keep off their Petitions; we must have
A Court-du-guard, I think, and Centries plac'd
At every dore.

ANGELLINA
I prethee let 'em enter.

[Enter **ANTONIO** disguised as a Petitioners with two other **PETITIONERS**.

FRANCESCINA
The room will not be sweet again this three days;
But if it be your pleasure—know your distance.

ANGELLINA
The blind, and lame, what's your condition Sir?

1ST PETITIONER
As miserable Madam as the Sea,
That swallow'd all my wealth, can make a man,

That once commanded thousands, I blush to beg
But Nature too impatient of sterving
Compels me to this boldness, you may soon
Peruse my tragick story there.

[Gives a Paper.

ANGELLINA
Good old man!

FRANCESCINA
What is his loss to you?

2ND PETITIONER
My Petition too;
A poor blind man, that hath lost more by fire
Than his estate valued a thousand times;
And 'tis but equall, fire should spoil my eyes,
That ravish'd me of all, was precious to 'em,
A wife and pretty Children.

ANGELLINA
Burn'd?

2ND PETITIONER
All burn'd;
And what my eyes cannot afford their memory
My poor heart weeps in bloud.

3RD PETITIONER
I am a Souldier
That in my Countries service lost my limbs;
I've had more lead in bullets taken from me
Than would repair some Steele.

FRANCESCINA
Ring the bells,
That was a loud one!

3RD PETITIONER
I have given wounds have kill'd the lookers on
With horror of their gaping, and have march'd
Ten miles a day thus deep—

FRANCESCINA
In dirt?

3RD PETITIONER

In blood.

FRANCESCINA
Upon those wooden leggs?

ANTONIO
Poor souls! I pitty 'em here honest men,
Divide this bag, and pray for my good Uncle.

OMNES
Blessings on you, Madam.

2ND PETITIONER
Equall division, come.

1ST PETITIONER
Stay, in the first place, I brought you hither,
Therefore my part is most considerable.

3RD PETITIONER
I'll have no Prerogative.

2ND PETITIONER
Nor I.

1ST PETITIONER
But I will.

[Throws off his disguise.

Do not I know you both for cheating Rascals?
Thus are good meanings cozen'd, and you sha'not
Lose your reward; send for some Officers.

2ND & 3 PETITIONERS
We are betray'd.

[Exit **2nd & 3rd PETITIONERS**

ANTONIO
My Uncle.

ANTONIO
They have found their eyes and leggs again,
Niece I observe your Charity, but you see not
The inside of these things, and I did mean
And hope these sums might serve your self;
Some Ladies would have considered

A new Gown and trinkets; Francescina,
I see little amendment, she'll undo me
In pious uses.

FRANCESCINA
She has entertain'd these Gentlewomen.

[Enter **VERGERIO**.

And that young Gentleman does good upon her.

ANTONIO
I like it well, he's carefull of my Lord,
And if she meet his honorable treaty,
She may learn Pride at Court, should our Art fail.
She smiles—I wo'not interrupt 'em.

[Enter **GIOIVANNI**.

GIOVANNI
My Lady entreats the presence of her Sister.

ANTONIO
Do's she entreat? Yes, you may visit her
Sir if you please, I'l trust her to your conduct.

VERGERIO
'Tis my ambition to attend her.

ANTONIO
Hark you,
Remember who you are, and carry things
For the credit of my heir, and one that must be
Right Honourable shortly, if I hear
Thou flout'st her, thou sha't have another Gown
And Petticoat embroider'd, or but beat her
And put me to a pension; fare you well,
Francescina wait, wait all upon you Mistress.

[Exeunt.

SCENE III

A Room in the Castle.

[Enter **PAULINA**.

PAULINA
No news yet of the Prince? he fill'd my dreams
Last night, it was a golden glorious slumber;
Me-thought we both were led into a Temple,
Where all our rites of Marriage were perform'd
In the presence of a thousand Angel-Cupids.

[Enter **PIPEROLLO** who stumbles.

PIPEROLLO
'Twas my devotion Madam, to present you
The News, I could not break my neck upon
A better cause.

PAULINA
Is the Prince come?

PIPEROLLO
The Prince is at your service; though I slipt
At Chamber door, it is my happiness
To be the first Messenger.

PAULINA
Of what?

PIPEROLLO
I desire no reward Madam, 'tis sufficient
I know what will become of us all, you
Remember the Caldean; all has happen'd,
I thank Astrology.

PAULINA
For what?

PIPEROLLO
Your money is gone, your rents have been received,
And my head broke to purpose; things are visible.

[Enter **LUCIO**.

My Master can confirm it.

PAULINA
What's this prodigie?

LUCIO
Madam 'tis done, we have been rob'd.

PAULINA
How?

LUCIO
As the Caldean and the Stars would have it,
Just to a minute.

PIPEROLLO
Rare Mathematician!

PAULINA
I'll hang you both,

PIPEROLLO
You may, and be no Princess.

PAULINA
Did he foretell this loss?

PIPEROLLO
Is my pate broken? Do I live, and hope
To kneel, and say, If please your Grace, to call
Him Lord, and answer to a Knight? -we 're made.

PAULINA
Be at a distance,
If there be truth in the Caldeans Art,
These inconsiderable losses are
A new presage of my approaching greatness.

[Enter **STEPHANIO** with **LONGINO**, disguized.

STEPHANIO
One from the Prince.

LONGINO
His Highness Farnese, Madam, greets your
Ladiship, and intends to be your Guest this night,

PAULINA
It will be an honour
My life must ow him duty for.

PIPEROLLO
Do not you feel a Lordship creep up
By your short ribs?

LONGINO
His Grace is not far off.

PAULINA
Present the humble duty of his handmaid,
And say my Castle droops til it receive him;

LONGINO
I shall Madam.

[Exit.

PAULINA
We must prepare to meet and entertain him;
All things have been Prophetical.

[Exit.

PIPEROLLO
My very good Lord.

LUCIO
Right Worshipfull Piperollo.

[Exeunt.

SCENE IV

The Approach to the Castle.

[Enter **VERGERIO**, **ANGELLINA**, **SERVANTS** aloof.

VERGERIO
In my pity
That so much innocence should not be lost
On faithless Contarini, I have landed
Upon your knowledge this unhappy secret.

ANGELLINA
Promis'd his faith to another? twas ill done,
To work my Uncle, and destroy my thoughts
Of a religious life.

VERGERIO
You may collect
Those pure desires again,

Heaven will be soon invited, and a second
Resolve confirm that happiness.

ANGELLINA
May we not,
Without so strict forsaking of the world,
Be capable of blessing, and meet heaven
At last, though erring Nature guide sometime
Out of the nearest way?

VERGERIO
Yes Angellina.

ANGELLINA
I must be no Votary,
But when you turn a Fryer then,

VERGERIO
How Lady?

ANTONIO
Sir you have merited for this discovery
All that I am to serve you, and unless
You help me in this Labyrinth, I must
Live in despair of Freedom.

VERGERIO
Any service;
There's so much sweetness in you, I could lay
My life a Sacrifice, be confident
I must be left of heaven, when I forsake you.

ANTONIO
And I dare trust your Virtue with a secret
I have not told my Ghostly Father.

FRAPOLO
I know not what opinion my Lord has
Of his smooth Advocate, but I should gather
By Symptomes of my Mistress, she is sick
Of the younger Gentleman.

VERGERIO
I dare not hope
This blessing, 'tis an honour plac'd on me
That has no value, I am a stranger,

ANTONIO

You are no stranger here.

VERGERIO
Your Uncle too—

ANGELLINA
May erre in his election.

VERGERIO
But his anger—

ANGELLINA
My prayer and tears may soften.

VERGERIO
Do not dress
Your eyes with sorrow Angellina, this
Too gracious an influence upon
Your servant must command my utmost duty.
Upon this white hand I breath out my heart,
And when I pay affection to another
Mistress, in Your revenge, her beauty blast me!
But we may be observ'd.

ANGELLINA
Be all my guide.

VERGERIO
This must be marriag'd wisely, we are lost els.

ANGELLINA
We are now arriv'd the Castle Francescina.

FRAPOLO
We attend.

[Exeunt.

SCENE V

Before the Castle.

[Enter **PRINCE FARNESE, CONTARINI**.

FARNESE
I am obscur'd sufficiently.

CONTARINI
My life on't.

FARNESE
Here are great preparations, and the people
Flock as to see some triumph, this Paulina
Will be ador'd i'th' Country.

CONTARINI
But her Sister,
With an extreme of sweetness, and humility
Will take the wonder off, she so transcends.

FARNESE
Your words fall from you,
I have observ'd my Lord, with too much passion;
She's but a woman, and may be no miracle,
When a clear eye is Judge.

CONTARINI
Sir I owe
All that I am in fortune, name and greatness
Unto your person, next whom, give me leave
To say I rate no expectation
Equall to be her servant, yet I find
Her cold to those desires, that court her with
All honour, I shall humbly beg, your grace
When you converse, will interpose your favour,
And by your Mediation perfect all
That can be nam'd my happiness.

FARNESE
You express
A strong Captivity in so small acquaintance;
Well my Lord trust to me; is this her Castle?

[Enter **PIPEROLLO**.

By your favour Sir.

PIPEROLLO
Speak quickly what's your business?

FARNESE
Is this Paulina's Castle?

PIPEROLLO

Plain Paulina? and is this her Castle?
My friend you want some breeding, she that owes
This Palace, for a Prince hath made it so,
Is not far off; turn your eyes backward Sir,
And tell your self without a perspective
What man is coming towards us?

FARNESE
Worthy Sir.

PIPEROLLO
Put of your hats and hear his name, Farnese
The Prince of Parma's there, I kist his hand,
My breath is since the sweeter.

FARNESE
The Prince, where?

PIPEROLLO
You'll find him with my Lady whom he came
To visit, if you'll promise to be drunk,
Take what's a secret yet, he comes to marry her,
Or ther's no truth in Stars, she is to be
His spouse; farewell, and thank my worship heartily.

[Exit.

CONTARINI
This fellow's mad!

FRAPOLO
He kist the Princes hand,
What mystery is this?

CONTARINI
See, they approach.

FARNESE
I am not lost sure in this cloud, they march
In State this way.

[Loud Musick.

[Enter in state, **FRAPOLO** disguised as the **PRINCE FARNESE,** leading in **PAULINA**, followed by **LONGINO,**
ANGELLINA, VERGERIO, LADIES and a Train of **GALLANTS**.

ANGELLINA
How, an Impostor?

VERGERIO
Sure I know the Prince.

ANGELLINA
Conceal it yet.

FARNESE
What Gentleman is that?

LONGINO
The Prince of Parma Sir.

CONTARINI
This will be worth observing.

FARNESE
Do we not both dream? that Paulina?
How disdainfully she moves?

CONTARINI
That's her younger Sister upon whom
Vergerio waits.

FARNESE
He knows I am the Prince.

CONTARINI
How do you like her Sir?

FARNESE [aside]
Ha! tis not fit to tell thee.

CONTARINI
Does she not answer my Character?

FARNESE
On my heart a fair one?

CONTARINI
Pray tell me how you like her Sir.

FARNESE
Not yet.
I am lost in wonder of her sweetness [aside] Bid
Vergerio bring her to Antonio's;
I'll be his guest to night.

CONTARINI
I shall obey Sir.

PIPEROLLO
Make room for the Prince, fellows bear back;
You are not to be Knighted friend I take it.

FARNESE
Thus can the flame of Heaven with subtill art,
Leave the skin whole, yet quite consume the heart.

[Exeunt.

ACT V

SCENE I

A Room in Antonio's House.

Enter **CONTARINI** and **ANTONIO**.

ANTONIO
MY Niece has had a pretty warm night on't,
'Tis a bold knave to take the Prince upon him
I did believe the noises, and was considering
How to contrive my peace with her good grace.

CONTARINI
You have no fear to suffer now?

ANTONIO
I thank
Your Lordship, that has made my house and knowledge
So fortunate, by the presence of our great
Farnese, 'tis an honour makes me young;
And yet this Rascal troubles me, that durst
Come in the Princes name, and charge my Niece
So home too; Is't not reason Sir?

CONTARINI
Of highest nature.

ANTONIO
Let him then tast the Law; yet I commend
His Spirit, that would scorn to die for Felonie,
And when his head goes off the shame and grief

May help to break her heart: I do not love her,
And then my Girl, my Angellina's heir,
And you her Lord and mine.

CONTARINI
My hopes are fair,
The Prince himself having vouchsaf'd to be
My Advocate.

ANTONIO
He must command all here.

[Enter **FARNESE** and **ANGELLINA**.

'Tis a good Prince, and loves you well, and let me
Without boast, tell you my Lord, she brings
No common Blood, though we live dark i'th' Country
I can derive her from the great Ursini—
But we have been eclips'd.

FARNESE
Contarini leave us.

[Exit **CONTARINI**.

You may stay Antonio;
Is't not an honour to your Family
A Prince should court your Niece into his arms?

ANTONIO
I must confess, 'tis good enough for such
A Baggage, they will make together Sir,
A most excellent shew upon the Scaffold.

FARNESE
The Impostor, and Paulina's pride, takes off
Your understanding; I do court your Niece
Fair Angellina.

ANTONIO
How Sir?

FARNESE
And as becomes a Princess.

ANTONIO
Your Grace is merry.

FARNESE
I know not, but there's Magick in her eyes.

ANTONIO
Magick? and she be a Witch, I ha' done with her.
Does he love Angelina? Please your Highness—
Do you affect this Girl?

FARNESE
Religiously.

ANTONIO
And have you all your Princely wits about ye?

FARNESE
This Language is but coarse. I tell you Sir
The Virgin must be mine.

ANTONIO
Your Whore?

FARNESE
My Princess.

ANTONIO
That's another matter.

FARNESE
Shew your obedience,
You have commands upon her as a Father.

ANTONIO
I know not what to say, but I'l perswade;
Hark you Neece, you hear what the Prince says,
'Tis now no time to think of Nunneries.
Be rul'd then, and love somebody; if you have
Promis'd my Lord, I say make good that promise,
If not, the Prince is worth considering.
The Gentleman will make you a round jointure.
If thou be'st free, love him, to vex thy Sister,
Who may upon submission be receiv'd
To Grace, and rise in time a Madam Nurse
To your heir apparent. I have done my duty.
But this is no great honesty, to cheat
My Lord. I see the greatest men are flesh
And blood, our souls are much upon a making;
All men that are in love deal with the Devil,
Only with this difference, he that dotes

Upon a Woman is absolutely possest;
And he that loves the least is haunted
With a Familiar.

[Enter a **SERVANT**

SERVANT
Old Fabio Sir your Tenant, with much business
In's face, desires to speak with you, I could hardly
Keep him from pressing in, his Wife he sayes
Is Lunatick.

ANTONIO
We shall all be mad shortly,
Where is the Knave?

[Exit **ANTONIO** and **SERVANT**.

ANGELLINA
I dare do Sir as much to shew my duty
As any Maid alive; I dare dye for you.

FARNESE
And yet you dare not love.

ANGELLINA
Not in that sense
You invite me to.

FARNESE
My Courtship carries
No stain to fright you, what I have propounded
Is worth the Ambition of a greater Lady;
Though you profess so liberally, I find
Your cunning, and because I have so much
Descended from my Title, you assume
This unbecomming Nicety, take heed,
I can be angry.

ANGELLINA
As you are a Man
That passion may come neer you Sir; and as
You are my Prince, you may command my death
To follow and Appease it, but you said you lov'd me.

FARNESE
I doe, if you can wisely entertain it.

ANTONIO
Then you must love my honor,
A Virgins wealth, for every honest Man
Or Woman has an honor, and that has
Engag'd my heart already by a Contract;
This tye dissolv'd with justice, I should kneel
To ask your Princely favour.

FARNESE
I am answer'd.
Who waits? call my Lord Contarini hither.

[Enter **CONTARINI**.

CONTARINI
Sir.

FARNESE
You might have mock'd another person,
And not have made me a ridiculous story
To your Mistress Sir.

CONTARINI
I understand you not.

FARNESE
Engage me to mediation for her love,
With a pretence how much my act should honor
Your faint hopes, when you are conscious of a
Contract, already past between you.

CONTARINI
Contract Sir?
She never yet gave me any language
Did promise hope, she still concluded me
With going to a Cloister.

FARNESE
How's this fair one?

ANTONIO
It is most sure I am contracted.

CONTARINI
To whom?

ANTONIO
Vergerio your Lordships Agent.

CONTARINI
That boy betray me?
In whom I took delight, made him my friend,
He play the Traytor? I'l be reveng'd upon
His heart.

FARNESE
Contain your passion Contarini,
Her beauty had apower above my friendship,
It well might shake his faith, and yet 'tis strange.
Call in Vergerio.

[Enter **VERGERIO**.

VERGERIO
I have heard all,
And come to meet my sentence. You're a Prince
'Gainst whom I dare not lift a thought; I see
What storm is rising, yet let this, great Sir,
Invite your mercy to me, I have made
No breach against your love, and that which was
My fault to his, may be excus'd, by what
He felt himself love, not to be resisted.
This Virgin I lay claim to, and her vowes
No Subject must compel me to resigne;
But if the Prince think me unfit, and call
This treasure from my bosome, and can place
His love, where I so chastly have delighted,
I will not keep a thought that shall repine,
When I am miserable in her absence,
But give my interest cheerfully; to you,
My Lord, I answer, I have made no trespass,
And shall, so please your highness to be judge,
Make it appear. [Whispers to the **DUKE**]

CONTARINI
Was ever such an impudence?
This presence does protect him, I should else
Write treason on his heart; But Angellina
I pity thy undoing, how canst thou
Expect a truth from him, betrays his Master?

ANTONIO
My Lord, you have been faulty sure, and this
(not worthy to be call'd a loss of me)
Was meant by Providence to wake your faith,
That's owing to another.

FARNESE
Possible?
The Vice-roy of Sicilies Daughter? Pulcheria.

CONTARINI
Pulcheria here?

VERGERIO
Here Contarini.

CONTARINI
Ha! prov'd a Woman, oh my shame and folly!

VERGERIO
Pardon my too much love, that made me fear
You had forgot Pulcheria, though you left
Your vowes and me at Sicily, when you were
Ambassadour from the Prince.

CONTARINI
Whence embarqu'd
Thou brought'st me news Pulcheria was dround,
And thou for her sake entertain'd my servant,
Welcome, at once receive me and forgive me.

FARNESE
I had your promise, were this contract void
In honour, nor will take from my own merit
To think when your considerate thoughts come home,
You can pretend excuse to your own happiness,
Which lest you may suspect, let us in state
Visit Paulina, and unmask that counterfeit
Which hath usurp'd our name.

VERGERIO
Sir we attend you,

CONTARINI
This blessing must require a spacious soul,
Mine is too narrow to receive.

[Exeunt.

SCENE II

An Outer Room in the Castle.

[Enter **STEWARD**, and **PIPEROLLO**.

LUCIO
I am not yet created honourable.

PIPEROLLO
Sir, things must have their time, but will his highness
Remove so suddenly, and carry my Lady
To th' Court with him? tis a most sweet young Prince.

LUCIO
Order was given to pack up her plate,
Her gold and Jewels, for he means to have
Tiltings and triumphs when he comes to Parma.

PIPEROLLO
There it is fit we should expect our honours.
I will attend the Prince.

[Exit.

[Enter **CONTARINI**

CONTARINI
Signior Lucio.

LUCIO
Your good Lordship.

CONTARINI
Pray tell my Lady, I would kiss her hand,
And shall present news will secure their welcome.
I come from the Prince.

LUCIO
The Prince my Lord?
He is within—

CONTARINI
A small march off the Castle, and commanded
Me to prepare her, that he comes to be
Her guest.

LUCIO
My Lord, I will acquaint some of the bed-chamber, but,
When did your Lordship see his Highness?

CONTARINI
I left him at the Park gate.

LUCIO
This is the nearest way unless his highness
Have leap'd a window, or can walk invisible.
Your Lordship may have some conceit. I'll go Sir.

[Exit.

[Enter **PIPEROLLO**.

PIPEROLLO
What is the meaning that ther's such a guard
Upon our Castle? 'tis besiedg'd, and no man
Suffer'd go forth; this is some Lord or other
By his stradling.

[Enter **LUCIO**, **LONGINO**, **STROZZO**, and the rest of the **BANDITTI**.

LONGINO
From the Prince? that he?

PIPEROLLO
'Tis as I tell you Sir, there's a little army,
Surrounds the Castle.

LONGINO
They have no order from his highness.

STROZZO
We are betraid agen.

LONGINO
Sir, would you speak with the Prince?

CONTARINI
Why have you such a thing within the Castle?
Who dares be so much Traitour to usurpe
That title? Wher's that Puppet, Gentlemen?

LUCIO
That is his Secretary.

PIPEROLLO
The rest are Lords and Privie Counsellors.

CONTARINI
We are undone.

[Enter **FARNESE, VERGERIO, ANGELLINA, ATTENDANTS**.

LONGINO
Tis he, the very he, I dare not look on him;
Oh for an impudence worth a Chronicle,
To outface him now, it were a possible thing,
If People would believe—

LUCIO
I'll tell my Lady, they are vanish'd; hum,
I do not like that face.

[Exit.

FARNESE
Come hither fellow, whom do you serve?

PIPEROLLO
I know not Sir.

FARNESE
What Prince have you within?

PIPEROLLO
The prince of Darkness.

FARNESE
What is this fellow?

PIPEROLLO
a Knight o'th' Post, the Pestle is too honourable.

FRAPOLO
Where is your Excellent Lady?

PIPEROLLO
I have a guess
If things go on, as I suspect, she will be—

FRAPOLO
Where?

PIPEROLLO
At her wits end very shortly.

FRAPOLO
An ingenious fellow?

PIPEROLLO
I have convers'd a little with the Mathematicks,
Sir, Who is that Gentlewoman, not that I am ignorant,
But to satisfie a doubt?

VERGERIO
She is one that may be
The Prince of Parma's Lady, when the Priest
Hath done his Office.

PIPEROLLO
If I be not mistaken
Here comes the Princesse, that is Angellina
The younger Sister.

[Enter **PAULINA**.

PAULINA
It is my wonder you that have the face
And garb of Gentlemen, should dare to be
So insolent, to affront our person,
And his, to whom your hearts and knees owe reverence.

FARNESE
Command the Impostor forth,
Seize on the Traitors.

[Enter **LONGINO**.

LONGINO
His Grace will be here presently, fear not Madam,
I would venter a Neck-breaking at some window,
And be content to crawl away a Cripple;
But there's no hope to scape the Multitude
That will be scrambling for my limbs. Great Sir,
I challenge the privilege of the last Bando,

[Kneels.

He that can bring Frapolo the chief Bandit,
Beside what was proclam'd other reward,
Shall have free pardon for all past-offences;
To that Grace I appeal, and here produce
Frapolo.

[Enter **FRAPOLO**, **STROZZO** and the rest of the **BANDITTI** &c.

PAULINA
This amazeth me.

FRAPOLO
Can you stand
The dazeling Sun so long, and not be struck
Blind for this bold affront? what wildness brought you
In multitudes to fright my happy peace,
And this good Ladies, my most vertuous Consort?

LONGINO
He bears up still!

FRAPOLO
Have all my cares and watchings to preserve
Your lives, and dearest liberties, deserv'd
This strange return, and at a time when most
Your happiness is concern'd, since by our Mariage
With this sweet Lady, full of grace and beauty,
You may expect an Heir to bless your Countrey.

CONTARINI
Will you suffer him?

FRAPOLO
'Tis time your Prince were dead, and when I am
Companion to my Fathers dust, these tumults
Fomented by seditious men, that are
Weary of Plenty, and delights of Peace,
Shall not approach to interrupt the calm
Good Princes after Death enjoy. Go home,
I pray depart, I rather will submit
To be depos'd, than wear a power or title
That shall not all be dedicate to serve you;
My life is but the gift of heaven, to wast it
For your dear sakes, my People are my Children,
Whom I am bound in Nature and Religion
To cherish and protect. Perhaps you have
Some grievance to present, you shall have justice
Against the proudest here; I look not on
Nobility of Birth. Office, or Fortunes,
The poorest subject has a Native Charter
And a Birth-right to th' Laws, and Common wealth,
Which with an equall, and impartial stream,
Shall flow to every bosom.

STROZZO
Pious Prince!

FARNESE
I am at a loss to hear him; sure I am
Farnese, if I be not lost by the way.

PIPEROLLO
Stand off Gentlemen,—let me see—which?
Hum! this—no, th'other. Hum! send for a Lion
And turn him loose, he wo'not hurt the true Prince.

FARNESE
Do not you know me Sir?

FRAPOLO
Yes, I know you too well, but it stands not
With my honor; what composition?

FARNESE
Who am I? Gentlemen, how dare ye suffer
This thing to talk? if I be your Farnese.

FRAPOLO
I say I am the Prince,

FARNESE
Prince of what?

FRAPOLO
Of Rogues, and please thy Excellence.

PAULINA
How?

FRAPOLO
You must excuse, I can hold out no longer
These were my Subjects Sir, and if they find
Your Mercy, I'm but one, whose head remov'd,
Or nooz'd, this Lady will be soon a Widdow,
Whom I have not deceiv'd, 'twas her Ambition
To go no less than Prince, and now you have one,
During this Gentlemans pleasure [To **PAULINA**].

PAULINA
What scorn shall I become?

FARNESE

Let him be guarded, and all his puppet. Lords.

[Enter **ANTONIO**, **FABIO**, **MORULLA**.

ANTONIO
News, news, excellent news; I shall leap
Out of my flesh for joy. Sir I have undertook
For your pardon to this reverend couple,
They heard my Niece was to be married
To the Prince, and thought it treason to conceal—

FARNESE
What?

ANTONIO
Paulina is not my Neece, no blood of mine;
Where is this Lady and her Pageant Prince?
The truth is, she is not Paulina, but their
Own Daughter.

FABIO
Possible? then we are both cheated.

ANTONIO
Whom she obtruded on our Family
When our Paulina died an Infant, with her,
A Nurse to both; Does your Grace apprehend?

FABIO
We do beseech your pardon.

ANTONIO
Now Angellina thou art heir to all.

PIPEROLLO
By all this Circumstance you are but my Sister!

CONTARINI
The Prince is prov'd a Prince of Theeves.

ANTONIO
Why ther's a Baggage and a Theef well met then.
I knew she was a Bastard, or a Changeling.

PAULINA
Where shall I hide my shame? O curst Ambition!

ANTONIO

Give you joy Sir, my most illustrious Nephew,
Joy to thy invisible Grace.

FRAPOLO
Thanks to our loving Uncle:

FARNESE
Take hence the Traitors.

ANGELLINA
Sir I beseech a pardon to their lives.
Let nothing of my story be remembered
With such a Tragedie, 'tis my first Petition.

FARNESE
I must not deny thee; all thank her Virtue;
Live you, and love that Gentlewoman; But
It were a sin to innocence, and our honor
Would encourage Treason by example,
If they should scape all Justice, take 'em to Custody:
Frapalo, we confine you to this Castle,
Where If she please your Bride may accompany you
Till we determine otherwise.

FRAPOLO
'Tis some mercy; but
I shall be getting Children, and two nothings
Wo'not maintain a Family, 'twere as good
To hang me out o'th' way, 'ere Charge come on,
Or take away my tools, I shall be working.

FARNESE
Provision shall be made you shall not sterve
Nor surfet Sir.

ANGELLINA
Because I call'd her Sister,
I will contribute something to their fortune.

FARNESE
What thy own goodness will direct; and now
Remove the Scene to Court, to perfect there
My own, and Parma's happiness; pride has
Met with severe reward, and that high justice
(That Governs all) though envy break with her
Own Poyson, calls the Amazed World to see
What blessings wait upon Humility.

[Exeunt.

FINIS.

EPILOGUE

FRAPOLO
Gentlemen, do not say you see me; I have made an escape from the Prince and Paulina; his graces word is but mortall, and not security enough for me; for all this Sun-shine he may hang me, when I come to Parma, for an example, and therefore I have chosen, rather to trust to my legs, than a reconcil'd State-Enemy.

Twil' not be worth your glory to betray
A man distrest, whom your own mercy may
Preserve to better service; rather then
Go back I'll stand your Justice Gentlemen.
I've plaid the thief, but you, as the case stands,
May save or kill, my life's now in your hands.

JAMES SHIRLEY – A CONCISE BIBLIOGRAPHY

The following includes years of first publication, and of performance if known, together with dates of licensing by the Master of the Revels if available.

TRAGEDIES
The Maid's Revenge (licensed 9th February 1626; printed, 1639)
The Traitor (licensed 4th May 1631; printed, 1635)
Love's Cruelty (licensed 14th November 1631; printed, 1640)
The Politician (acted, 1639; printed, 1655)
The Cardinal (licensed 25th May 1641; printed, 1652).

TRAGI-COMEDIES
The Grateful Servant (licensed 3rd November 1629 as The Faithful Servant; printed 1630)
The Young Admiral (licensed 3rd July 1633; printed 1637)
The Coronation (licensed 6th February 1635, as Shirley's, but printed in 1640 as a work of John Fletcher)
The Duke's Mistress (licensed 18th January 1636; printed 1638)
The Gentleman of Venice (licensed 30th October 1639; printed 1655)
The Doubtful Heir (printed 1652), licensed as Rosania, or Love's Victory in 1640
The Imposture (licensed 10th November 1640; printed 1652)
The Court Secret (printed 1653).

COMEDIES
Love Tricks, or the School of Complement (licensed 10th February 1625; printed under its subtitle, 1631)
The Wedding (ca. 1626; printed 1629)

The Brothers (licensed 4th November 1626; printed 1652)
The Witty Fair One (licensed 3rd October 1628; printed 1633)
The Humorous Courtier (licensed 17th May 1631; printed 1640).
The Changes, or Love in a Maze (licensed 10th January 1632; printed 1639)
Hyde Park (licensed 20th April 1632; printed 1637)
The Ball (licensed 16th November 1632; printed 1639)
The Bird in a Cage, or The Beauties (licensed 21st January 1633; printed 1633)
The Gamester (licensed 11th November 1633; printed 1637)
The Example (licensed 24th June 1634; printed 1637)
The Opportunity (licensed 29th November 1634; printed 1640)
The Lady of Pleasure (licensed 15th October 1635; printed 1637)
The Royal Master (acted and printed 1638)
The Constant Maid, or Love Will Find Out the Way (printed 1640)
The Sisters (licensed 26th April 1642; printed 1653).
Honoria and Mammon (printed 1659)

DRAMAS
A Contention for Honor and Riches (printed 1633), morality play
The Triumph of Peace (licensed 3rd February 1634; printed 1634), masque
The Arcadia (printed 1640), pastoral tragicomedy
St. Patrick for Ireland (printed 1640), neo-miracle play
The Triumph of Beauty (ca. 1640; printed 1646), masque
The Contention of Ajax and Ulysses (printed 1659), entertainment
Cupid and Death (performed 26th March 1653; printed 1659), masque